PINTEREST
MARKETING
BIBLE

THE DEFINITIVE GUIDE TO MARKETING
YOUR BRAND AND PRODUCTS
ON PINTEREST

BY LEON CHO

Pinterest Marketing Bible

The Definitive Guide to Marketing Your Brand and Products on Pinterest

 TURNRAMP PRESS

ISBN-13: 978-0615599335

V1.0

For Tina
my inspiration for everything

Contents

Introduction

What?! Yet *another* social network?

Whether you're a community manager, CMO, social media expert, blogger, brand marketer, or selling your own jewelry online, you're probably suffering from the dreaded condition known as 'Social Media Fatigue.' The last few years have brought an explosion of new social networks and tools. You're still juggling Facebook, Twitter, YouTube, Google+, LinkedIn, Digg... and now everybody's suddenly talking about Pinterest.

There's no denying that social media has completely transformed marketing. But you're right to be reluctant to jump on the bandwagon for every new social network. That is, of course, unless it's really can help you achieve things you can't already do with all the other social media. It would be worth your time if the new social network allows you to reach a large and still underserved demographic, deliver your brand message in more emotional ways, or automatically target the affinity groups that will be most passionate about your products. And it would definitely be worth it if it can drive meaningful sales and traffic.

Yes, Pinterest can do all of these things. If you're reading this book, you are one of the first to recognize that Pinterest is not just a "me too" social network. It works in completely different ways that are appealing to women and families, is centered around visual images rather than text, and has users who have self-identified their interests and are actively looking for your products rather than the other way around.

Don't let the lack of overt advertising on Pinterest fool you. There is a lot of marketing already going on within Pinterest if you know where to look for it. Pinterest is already generating meaningful traffic and sales for those brands, companies, and individuals that know how to market effectively in this new model. In many ways, Pinterest's design makes for a better marketing platform than other social networks.

And don't worry, the customers will be there too. According to Hitwise data, Pinterest is already one of the top 10 social networks and has passed Google+ in visits. The users are some of the most engaged on the web with the average site visit lasting a staggering 15 minutes. Famed investor Ron Conway has compared Pinterest's user growth to Facebook in 2006.

To allow you take advantage of this opportunity as quickly as possible, we'll cover all aspects of strategy and tactics. Once you truly understand why Pinterest is different and how it works, we'll put together a quick strategic brief for your business that won't compromise your ability to remain nimble. Then, you'll learn specific tactics including board organization, pin content and copy, getting followers, and tools.

With this information, you'll have a great head start on Pinterest which is quickly becoming an essential marketing channel for anyone working or using social media and online marketing. Once you have this foundation, you'll also be able to join the Pinterest marketing community on PinBliss.com as we learn and share together.

CHAPTER 1: UNDERSTANDING PINTEREST

What Exactly Is Pinterest?

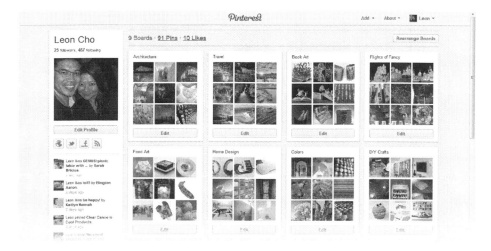

Pinterest has been described many different ways including an online pinboard, visual bookmarking, a personalized magazine, and visual scapbooking. I like to compare Pinterest to a real-world cork board or bulletin board that you hang in your room. Every time you find something particularly inspiring or beautiful on the web, you take a photo of it and pin it up on your cork board. Your board becomes a place where you collect and organize all the wonderful things you find on the web. Of course, you'll want to organize your photos too. You might group together photos of all the design ideas for your dream house, all the wondrous electronic gadgets you wish you had, and photos of flowers that you want to draw on for inspiration in planning your future wedding. Over time, your corkboard is neatly organized to capture many of your interests and dreams.

Now imagine that everyone in the world has their own corkboard in their room. Pinterest gives you the ability to not only manage your own board but also to see everyone else's board. You can find other people who have the same hobbies and interests that you do and draw from their board for inspiration. You can even directly copy their pins and put them on your own board to make it more complete.

Already, this sounds very different from Facebook, Twitter, and LinkedIn. But we are going to see how profoundly different this really is from other social media. We'll study in detail why this appeals to a different audience and how it opens up entirely new ways of marketing brands and products. The opportunities are very big but so are the potential traps and pitfalls which we seek to avoid by deeply understanding this new model for social networking.

Can Pinterest Be Used for Marketing?

You may have noticed that Pinterest is remarkably ad-free. It doesn't appear to have many of the typical forms of online advertising like banner ads on the site, sponsored links in the search results, or images marked as ads in your scrolling feed of images. When you scroll down your feed of Pinterest images, you rarely see a brand logo or name anywhere. In fact, the only hint that some sort of marketing might be happening behind the scenes is the "Gifts" menu that allows you to search for gifts by price range.

Pinterest is such a fundamentally different model that most Pinterest users are unaware that marketing is happening on the site even when it alters their perception of brands or influences a transaction. In reality, Pinterest is perfect for marketing precisely because Pinterest users don't feel bombarded by overt advertising. They voluntary share their interests and are self-motivated to reach out and discover great new products and services that match their interests. Because they choose it rather than having it aggressively pushed at them, they don't feel they are being sold anything. The early adopters of Pinterest who are able to understand the new model are reaping the benefits. Do not be fooled by the lack of display ads -- there is a lot of marketing already happening on Pinterest.

Here is how Pinterest is being used for marketing:

- **Brand Awareness**. Through photos and videos, you have the opportunity to showcase your brand values and your products. As we'll see, there are fewer privacy concerns on Pinterest so your photos will reach more people since Pinterest users are willing to share exciting pins with total strangers. Also, Pinterest users see pins based on self-selected interests so your images touch a targeted audience that will be more likely to be passionate about your brand.

- **Sales or affiliate commissions**. Yes, people are already directly selling products on Pinterest. When you see a pin with an image of a really cool product or service, you can click through to a web page. Typically, this link will take you to a web page where you can get more information or make a purchase. Even affiliate links work on Pinterest so it's possible for you to earn commissions using Pinterest to distribute products for other companies as well.

- **Product testing/evaluation**. Pinterest has the potential to be a giant focus group. Since Pinterest is so visual, you can share photos of multiple concept designs to ask for comments or just to see what people share the most by repining.

- **Drive traffic**. Pinterest can work together with your other social media initiatives and websites to help you drive traffic. You can link images on Pinterest pins anywhere – including to your Facebook page or your website. For the time being, links from Pinterest are even "do follow" links that can boost your search engine ranking.

How Is Pinterest Different From Other Social Networks?

There must be something different about Pinterest. After all, with so many choices for social networks including Facebook, Google+, LinkedIn, Path, and Twitter, why are so many people willing to sign up for yet another social network? We'll also see that Pinterest has attracted more women than men. What is it that makes Pinterest so special?

- **More Emotional**. The first thing everyone says about Pinterest is that it's "visual." That's the most obvious difference. But what they're really saying is that Pinterest connects on a more sensory, emotional level than the other websites and social networks that are covered in text. When you go to Facebook, Twitter, and blogs, you see pages of words. Since you are mostly reading, visiting those sites is a cerebral experience where you have to absorb and think about information. Pinterest is visceral. We instinctively react to the colors, shapes, and stunning beauty of photos. You will see that this difference is one of the keys to how we market effectively on Pinterest.

- **Less social anxiety**. At first, it may seem like a negative rather than a positive that Pinterest is less social than other social networks. After spending some time on Pinterest, you'll realize that there is not a lot of conversation on the site despite the ability to write comments. The interactions between users are largely done by sharing images and video rather than talking about them. But with the conversation gone, so is the social anxiety. There's no pressure to remember birthdays, respond to messages in your inbox, or comment on a friend's subtle cry for attention. There's no relationship drama being played out in public. Pinterest connects people in a new way through interests rather than dialogue.

- **Feels safer**. Because you are sharing your interests on Pinterest and not your personal life, there are far fewer privacy concerns. Other Pinterest users can see from your profile that you are passionately interested in cooking and shoes – not review embarrassing photos from that party two years ago when your friend had way too much to drink. This creates the potential for you to connect with more people because you don't mind sharing your Pinterest boards with complete strangers.

- **Goes at my pace**. Many social networks give you a real-time stream of what's going on right now. There are tweets on live news as it happens, Foursquare check-ins broadcasting where your friends are right now, and Facebook status updates from the party still in progress. This means that you also have to check Facebook and Twitter all day long to keep up even if it's while you're on vacation, at the dinner table, or in a meeting. Pinterest doesn't have the same expiration date on its content. People are sharing their interests rather than live news. This makes Pinterest a much more relaxed experience where you don't feel rushed or guilty if you don't come back for a few days. As you'll see from the engagement statistics, Pinterest users are still extremely active on the site but they don't feel stressed by the urgency of using it.

- **Outlet for creative expression without the work**. Everyone needs a creative outlet but not everyone has the time or creative genius to author masterful works of art from scratch. However, everyone has an opinion. If you ask someone truly passionate about cooking, you'll hear strong views on the absolute best kitchen gadget, the indisputably right way to cut an onion, or the only authentic way to make lasagna. All of us are happy to share our expertise and passions with others and even if we don't have time to create, we can curate.

- **Aspirational**. Most social networks serve as a way to express yourself. But while Facebook is where you express who you are now (and who you were in the past), Pinterest is very much about who you want to be in the future. Although every user can create and categorize their boards any way they want, some of the frequently seen boards contain images for a user's dream home, perfect wedding, or fantasy travel destinations. Your Pinterest boards are not necessarily so much a reflection of who you are now as the person you will be someday.

Why Marketing on Pinterest is Different

Now that we understand how Pinterest is different from other social media from the perspective of the Pinterest user, what does this mean for marketing? We've seen that Pinterest works in a fundamentally different way than Facebook and Twitter. It's more emotional, anchored by interests rather than conversation, and more aspirational. These differences open up some completely new ways to approach marketing that would not work in other marketing channels.

- **People with the right affinities find you**. This is backwards from how marketing usually works. Typically, you start by identifying the interests or affinities of people who are most likely to purchase your products. Then, you find out where those people are and you reach out to them. On Pinterest, the right audience finds you. They self-identify their interests through the choices they make about which boards to create and follow. Then, they are self-motivated to scour the Pinterest site looking for things that fit with their interests to pin on their board. Of course, there are still important tactics you can use in the "Pinterest Marketing Tactics" section to help more people find you, but the Pinterest model can be very advantageous to marketers.

- **You can connect more emotionally through images**. Research has shown that the majority of purchase decisions are driven by emotion rather than logic. On Pinterest, you won't be tempted to try to explain your product with logic because Pinterest doesn't give you a lot of room to write text. You essentially have only a visual image to stir emotional curiosity and sensory excitement. If you can do this well enough to stand out in a sea of other photos on Pinterest, you will have created an emotional connection that will be hard to shake – even when your audience starts to evaluate other competitors with logic.

- **Your content will be shared further**. People on Pinterest share their interests, not their personal life. This means far fewer privacy concerns and a willingness to share great pins or connect with other Pinterest users who are complete strangers.

- **You can market a lifestyle, not a product**. You are marketing a lifestyle. Even if all you sell right now are wedding gowns, you can still pin images of flowers, wedding cakes, hair, and other design inspiration for the perfect wedding. This will give you the ability to expand your product and service offerings in the future and to associate your brand with a larger, aspirational vision.

- **Reaches underserved demographic of women and their families**. As you can see from the "Pinterest Demographics" section, a large majority of Pinterest users are women. Women feel underserved by existing advertising and Pinterests represents a tremendous opportunity to communicate with them more effectively. In fact, 91% of women say that advertisers don't understand them (Greenfield Online for Arnold's Women's Insight Team) yet they account for 85% of all consumer purchases from homes to autos to healthcare (Marketing to Women conference).

Pinterest Reach and Growth

Pinterest is spreading like wildfire. Since launching in March 2010, Pinterest became one of the top social networks in only months. By January 2012, it was the 7th most visited social networking site (Hitwise) putting it ahead of Google+ and behind only large networks like Facebook, YouTube, Twitter, and LinkedIn. In December 2011, Pinterest.com had

7.21M unique visitors (Compete.com). Even more revealing about its marketing potential, a study of 5 specialty apparel retailers by Monetate showed same-store referral traffic from Pinterest rising 389% in the 6-month period from July to December2011.

And Pinterest's explosive growth shows no sign of slowing down. Famed investor Ron Conway compared Pinterest user growth to Facebook in 2006. Yet, Pinterest started small. Very few people had taken notice of Pinterest in November 2010 when, 8 months after launch, it had only accumulated 40K users. It then proceeded to grow from those 40K users to 3.3M in just one year. Looking back, Pinterest has grown 50% month over month from inception to November 2011 and is expected to grow to 30M users by Nov 2012 (Steve Cheney, Tech Crunch, "How to Make Your Startup Go Viral The Pinterest Way", November 2011).

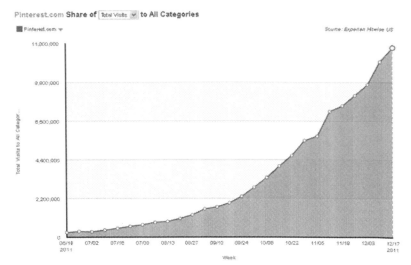

Source: Experian Hitwise, December 2011

Pinterest's viral growth is also being facilitated by new tools. Pinterest makes it easy to create buttons on external websites asking people to pin content and follow people on Pinterest. Pinterest was also a launch partner of Facebook's Open Graph platform which allows activity on Pinterest to be published to a user's Facebook news feed.

Lastly, we should mention that Pinterest is not only acquiring a lot of users but that those users are also very actively using the service. The average time on site for Pinterest is an extremely high 15+ minutes (Google's Doubleclick Ad Planner, January 2012).

Pinterest Demographics

So who is the Pinterest user? The demographics look very different from other popular social networking sites:

- **Mostly Female** (80% female, 20% male).
- **Age 25 to 54** (80% of total with 27% age 25-34, 29% age 35-44, 24% age 45-54)
- **Did not complete college** (only 25% have a Bachelor's degree or higher)
- **Annual household income of $25K-75K** (69% of total with 35% $25K-$49K, 34% $50K-$75K)

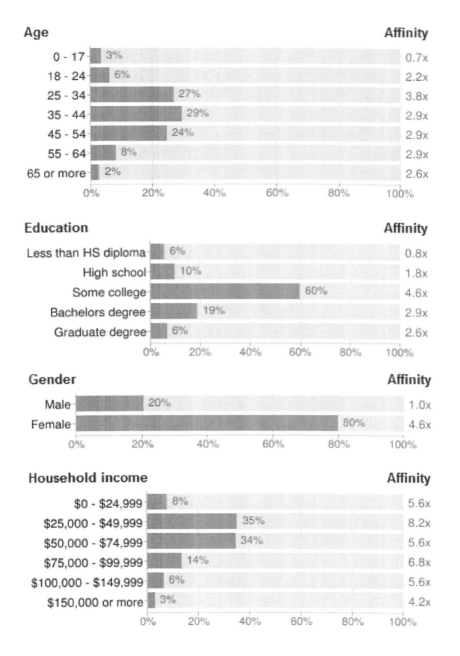

Age   Affinity

Age	Percent	Affinity
0 - 17	3%	0.7x
18 - 24	6%	2.2x
25 - 34	27%	3.8x
35 - 44	29%	2.9x
45 - 54	24%	2.9x
55 - 64	8%	2.9x
65 or more	2%	2.6x

Education   Affinity

Education	Percent	Affinity
Less than HS diploma	6%	0.8x
High school	10%	1.8x
Some college	60%	4.6x
Bachelors degree	19%	2.9x
Graduate degree	6%	2.6x

Gender   Affinity

Gender	Percent	Affinity
Male	20%	1.0x
Female	80%	4.6x

Household income   Affinity

Household income	Percent	Affinity
$0 - $24,999	8%	5.6x
$25,000 - $49,999	35%	8.2x
$50,000 - $74,999	34%	5.6x
$75,000 - $99,999	14%	6.8x
$100,000 - $149,999	6%	5.6x
$150,000 or more	3%	4.2x

Source: Doubleclick Ad Planner by Google, December 2011

Experian Hitwise data from December 2011 shows that the U.S. demographic falls into predominantly into 3 Mosaic lifestyle segments:

- Boomers and Boomerangs – Baby boomer adults (age in 50's and 60's) and their young adult children (teens and 20's) who are still living in the same suburban home. This group has conservative values and is family-oriented. They are heavy web users and consume a lot of media.
- Babies and Bliss – These are parents of large families (5 or more people in the household) living in the suburbs. Parents are in the 30's and 40's and kids span ages from preschool to high school. This is a wealthier group with low six-figure incomes from dual earner households. However, with the large family, they are still value-conscious despite more upscale tastes. With their busy lifestyles, they also care more about convenience. Again, a group with conservative and family values.
- Families Matter Most - These are young, middle-class families in the suburbs. They are proud of their new homes and their newly adopted skills for juggling work and raising their kids. They are price-sensitive and less impulsive in their shopping purchases.

Across all of these groups, we see a focus on family and conservative values. The Pinterest demographic centers their life around home, children, and family life. They are value-conscious in the products they purchase. We see validation for this on the Pinterest site by the popularity of pins for home furnishings, home décor, recipes, time-saving household tips, and ideas for kid's games and craft projects.

What Brands, Products, and Services Can You Most Effectively Promote on Pinterest?

There are certain things that can be promoted more effectively on Pinterest than on Facebook, Twitter, and YouTube. But there are also certain things that are more difficult to market. Not every brand and certainly not every product in your catalog is a good fit for Pinterest. So which brands, products, and services appeal to this demographic? What can most effectively be promoted or sold with the marketing approaches you will be using on Pinterest?

While a brand, product, or service doesn't necessarily need to match all of the following criteria to be successful, you want as many of the following characteristics as possible:

- **You can see what separates you from the competition.** There are successful brands that differentiate solely on price, availability/selection, support, or durability. But if that's all that separates you from the competition, you'll have a much harder time promoting it on Pinterest than a competitor differentiating on style and product design. Pinterest is all about images and what you can see with your eyes. However, don't discount Pinterest as a solution if you differentiate on service as long as you can capture emotionally compelling images of people being treated to unique and unexpected experiences or personal attention.
- **It's unique.** On Pinterest, your pins will be just one image among hundreds that a user scrolls through in a session with Pinterest. Your product won't get noticed or shared if it's commonplace. It needs to be something out of the ordinary, something distinctive.
- **Appeals to demographic of women and families.** Given the unique demographics of Pinterest, does your brand appeal to women? How do your products and services fit with the challenges and joys of raising a family?
- **The appeal is emotional.** Imagine looking at a photo of one of your products or a photo of people using your service. What do you feel? Does it trigger a sensory reaction? Pinterest connects with people on an emotional level rather than an intellectual one.
- **The size of your brand doesn't matter.** Pinterest levels the playing field. Whether you're selling handmade crafts from your garage or you're a big company, everyone is just an image in the Pinterest gallery. Pinterest offers the opportunity for small brands to be discovered and for large brands to give exposure to more niche products that may not have the distribution of the top sellers.

- **Aspirational**. Are you selling a better life? Pinterest users are pinning inspiration for the life they want someday – the dream home, the exotic vacations they are anticipating, the fantasy wedding, and the perfect dinner party. Do your brand and products help people achieve that higher vision of themselves?

For example, here are some popular product and service categories for pins that meet the criteria above:

- Arts & craft projects
- Hair & makeup products
- Media (TV shows, movies, music, books)
- Fitness products and training programs
- Women's apparel
- Jewelry & fashion accessories
- Gardening supplies
- Furniture and home décor
- Time-saving products and activities for kids
- Baby products
- Affinity products for pet lovers
- Art (prints, posters)
- Travel destinations and experiences
- Gadgets and style accessories
- Diets
- Party and entertainment products
- Wedding products and services
- Personal motivation
- Lifestyle and parenting tips
- Family games
- Kitchen appliances
- Unique household products
- Recipes
- Housewares

Given the broad interests of the demographic, there are inevitably more categories that will emerge. However, if you are introducing a new category that does not already have a following on Pinterest, it is recommended that you look for ways to at least partially tap into some of the existing categories. Pinterest users repin what fits into one of their existing boards. If it defies categorization for them, it may be a more uphill climb to build a following.

CHAPTER 2: PINTEREST MARKETING STRATEGY

Steps for Developing a Marketing Strategy

Pinterest is just part of your social media strategy, not your entire strategy. At this stage in Pinterest's growth, it's also likely that you don't have a huge team dedicated to Pinterest --- it's going to be an additional responsibility for your social media team or it may very well be just you.

The greatest contributor to success at this stage of Pinterest's rapid growth is your ability to remain nimble. So the last thing you need is an exhaustive strategy session building complex plans that will almost certainly change. Instead, we recommend that you build a laser-focused, one or two page document that crystallizes your goals, engagement plan, integration plan, and metrics. We want you to get started quickly. You'll only learn what works best for your brands and products by doing – not drawing up more detailed plans.

Your plan should focus on strategy rather than tactics. We'll go into detail on tactics in a later section so you will be prepared to execute on your strategy. For now, your focus is understanding what you want to accomplish on Pinterest and a rough idea of how Pinterest fits with your specific brand, products, and services.

Here's what should be covered in your "Pinterest Marketing Strategy Brief":

- **Define your business goal for Pinterest**. What do you want to accomplish? Don't start with a Pinterest-focused metric like "get X number of followers or clicks from Pinterest." You need to start with a business goal. What business result do you want from marketing on Pinterest? Are you trying to build brand awareness, increase affiliate sales, market test new product concepts, get more traffic, or directly drive sales?

- **Define success metrics**. Based on your business goal, how will you measure it? What level of traffic, sales, or signups would constitute success?

- **Education/Training**. How will you educate management and the other stakeholders on the importance of Pinterest? How will you train the people with day-to-day responsibilities for Pinterest marketing activities? One easy way to do this is simply to get copies of this book for everyone on your social media team and management. But no matter how you choose to educate your team and stakeholders, make sure everybody understands the magnitude of the opportunity and how marketing on Pinterest is different from other social networks. Of course, don't forget to get everyone signed up for a Pinterest account and using it!

- **Engagement Plan**. What will you actually do on Pinterest to achieve your goals? On a regular basis, you will be coming up with new ideas for campaigns and ways to improve performance so you shouldn't feel that you need to forecast everything you plan to do for the next year.

  o Content Strategy. Not all of your brands or everything in your product catalog is a good fit fo Pinterest. Which ones are most likely to be successful? Refer back to "What brands, products, and services can you most effectively promote on Pinterest?" section for criteria to assist with this process.

  o **Integration Strategy**. How can your other online properties or teams work together to promote Pinterest? Pinterest does not exist in a vacuum. You will want to cross-promote your Pinterest boards and profile with the communities you have already built on your websites and other social media. In the section on "Getting Followers with Other Channels" we go into more detail on specific techniques for integration.

  ○ **Campaign Strategy**. What promotional campaigns can help you get more followers on Pinterest? Create an initial list of ideas is for campaigns that you could run on Pinterest to achieve your business goals. Refer to the list of "Campaign Ideas" in the next section for some different approaches.

- **Reporting**. In order to track your marketing efforts, you need to consider what you can measure. Can you measure traffic referrals from Pinterest.com? Can you measure sales through specific affiliate or referral codes that you use in your Pinterest links? Can you report on progress in the number of repins and followers? Chances are good that you already have most of these basic statistics available through existing web analytics tools but you should highlight anything here that requires development work to implement or automate. You should also have a regular schedule for reporting to be sure that you able to monitor the results of your campaigns and strategies and respond quickly.

- **Tools**. At this time, most of the tools you will need will be in the "Pinterest Tools" section. You will likely also utilize your existing web analytics tools or a free web analytics service like Google Analytics to help you track referral traffic from Pinterest.

Campaign Ideas

In addition to the many marketing tactics that we discuss in the "Pinterest Marketing Tactics" section, you may want to experiment with running promotional campaigns on Pinterest in order to get more followers or attention to your boards. Here are a few basic ideas that span the full range of business goals:

- **Photo Contests**. Let the Pinterest community help you create creative and unique photos of your product or category. Run a photo contest with prizes that challenges participants to take a photo of themselves using your product in exotic locations, using your product in an unusual way, or submitting humorous photos. Post the winners to a Pinterest board with links back to your website.

- **Caption/Slogan Contests**. Post a provocative photo involving your product or category to your Pinterest board and challenge the Pinterest community to comment with a caption or slogan. Award a prize for the best one.

- **Product Focus Group**. Post photos of new product designs or ideas and get feedback from the Pinterest community before committing the time and resources to fully implement them. Let people vote with likes or repins.

Case Studies

In this section, we examine a number of case studies of Pinterest done right. This is not intended to be a comprehensive survey of all the top Pinterest boards. Rather, we intentionally focus only a few boards that are doing some aspect of Pinterest marketing particularly well.

It should be noted that there are many Pinterest accounts with a large number of followers simply because they have massive brand awareness through advertising, retail store locations, or website traffic. In other cases, certain brands on Pinterest may have a large number of original pins because they are in the business of generating content for a print magazine or website and have staff for creating content for other channels. Again, our goal is not to be comprehensive but to learn from a few best practices.

- **Whole Foods**

- o Category: Grocery

- o Pinterest URL: pinterest.com/wholefoods

- o What to Note: This is a great example of using Pinterest to promote your brand without a focus on driving sales. All of the boards are aligned with the brand focus around natural living and food but, interestingly, almost none explicitly feature branded Whole Foods products. Instead, the boards reflect the aspirational lifestyle of the Whole Foods customer that entertains friends with delicious meals and is socially conscious. Pins include elaborate celebrations with food, beautiful kitchens, gardens, and environmental tips.

- **Real Simple**

- o Category: Media

- o Pinterest URL: pinterest.com/realsimple

- o What to Note: Real Simple's content is well aligned with many
  of the most popular categories on Pinterest – recipes, craft
  ideas, decorating tips, fashion, and home décor. Pinterest is
  used to drive traffic to the realsimple.com website but

website users are also connected back to Pinterest with the "Pin It" button featured on most pages. Real Simple also demonstrates how a brand's image can be reinforced by using a consistent visual style across photos. Many of the photos have plain white backgrounds which give the Pinterest boards the same visual aesthetic of minimalist simplicity as the print magazine.

- **Etsy**

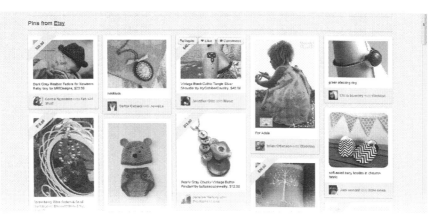

Item

♥ Add item to favorites

💝 See who favorites this item

2555 views

246 admirers

81 Treasury lists

$60.00 USD

🛒 | Add to Cart   ♥ Favorite

Only 1 available

o   Category: Handmade/Vintage, Arts & Crafts

o   Pinterest URL: pinterest.com/source/etsy.com,
    pinterest.com/etsy

o   What to Note: What's important is not Etsy's own Pinterest or
    the efforts of its marketing staff. Rather, Etsy's success on
    Pinterest is the result of efforts by its individual community
    members to take advantage of Pinterest as a platform to sell
    their own handmade and vintage products. Etsy has
    facilitated this with a "Pin It" button on their website.
    However, Etsy's success can most likely be attributed to the
    strong alignment with the Pinterest demographic (Etsy sellers
    and Pinterest users are mostly women) and the product fit

between Etsy's unique and limited handmade products and the interest in arts and crafts on Pinterest. As Etsy provides the tools for someone to sell their own handmade products online, there is a built-in financial incentive for Etsy users to utilize Pinterest to expose their products to more buyers.

- **West Elm**

  - Category: Furniture, Home Decor

  - Pinterest URL: pinterest.com/westelm

  - What to Note: Rather than organizing boards by product categories, boards are organized by styles (Modernist, Naturalist, Globalist, Revivalist, etc.). This allows Pinterest users to follow boards that match their personal style while allowing West Elm to help their followers discover a wide variety of products within a particular style. They also pin a large amount of design inspiration images drawn from around the web – not just their own products.

- **Bergdorf Goodman**

o   Category: Fashion

o   Pinterest URL: pinterest.com/bergdorfs

o   What to Note: Boards are created around specific fashion
    trends in the current season (eg. Prints, Tribal, Black & White).
    The board organization now actually provides a way for
    Pinterest users to learn about current fasion trends through
    the board descriptions. In this way, Pinterest users also self-
    select the styles that appeal most to them and Bergdorf
    Goodman can effectively personalize the products showcased
    to each follower.

- **ShopItToMe**

- o Category: Fashion, Personalized Search/Deals

- o Pinterest URL: pinterest.com/shopittome

- o What to Note: Boards include pins from around the web, not just their own products. ShopItToMe has a dedicated board for their own products but also boards with inspiring fashion-related items including apparel, accessories, and makeup.

- **Nordstrom**

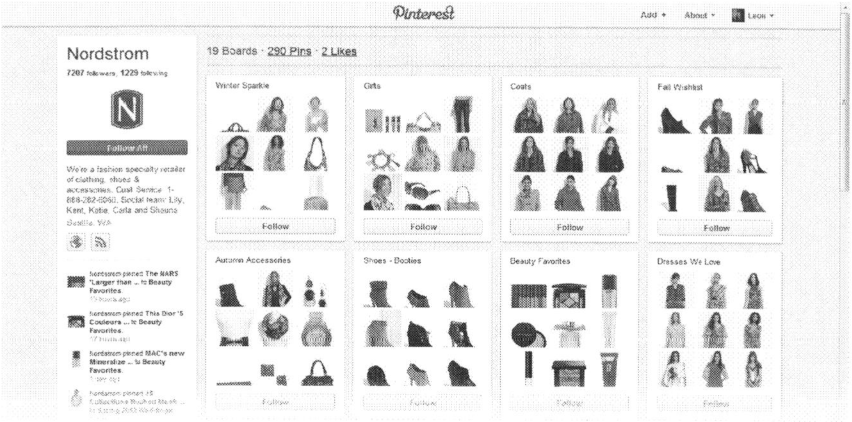

o   Category: Retail, Fashion

o   Pinterest URL: pinterest.com/nordstrom

o   What to Note: Boards are well organized by product category
    and seasons which makes it easy to follow only the boards
    that matter to you. Reflecting Nordstrom's brand
    commitment to customer service, they also publish a
    telephone number and the names of the social media team
    curating the Pinterest boards.

●   **Time Magazine**

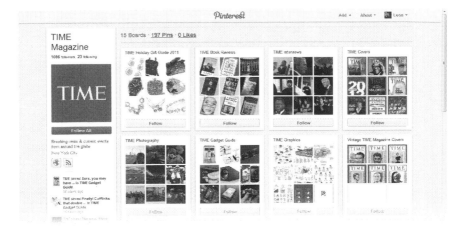

- o Category: Media

- o Pinterest URL: pinterest.com/time_magazine

- o What to Note: Rather than trying to directly translate their site their site to Pinterest with breaking news stories, site focuses on more enduring content such as infographics, photography, product reviews, historical magazine covers, and celebrities. Content has broad appeal (movies, music, fashion) and visual impact.

- **Cabot Cheese**

- o Category: Food

- o Pinterest URL: pinterest.com/cabotcheese

- o What to Note: Rather than just direct photos of their products, they take advantage of the strong interest in recipes within the Pinterest community and focus on pins of recipes that use their cheese products. The recipes are beautifully photographed. Cabot Cheese also reinforces their brand image as a New England family farm with photos for farmers, Vermont, and New England.

- **Cooking Light**

o Category: Media, Cooking

o Pinterest URL: pinterest.com/cookinglight

o What to Note: Cooking Light ran a "Superfast Fan of the Month" competition where people would blog about the experience of using a Cooking Light recipe. The winners were posted into a "Superfast Fans" Pinterest board which allowed Cooking Light to link to web pages from readers which served as effective testimonials for their recipes. This highlights the potential value of pinning content not just from your own site but leveraging content generated by your customers and community that may be even more effective in promoting your brand.

• **Chris March (Mad Fashion on Bravo TV)**

- ○ Category: Media, Media Personality

- ○ Pinterest URL: pinterest.com/chrismarch

- ○ What to Note: As a way of promoting the Mad Fashion TV show on Bravo, Chris March posts fashions and style inspirations from each episode of the show. Each image links back to the corresponding episode blog or photo gallery on the bravotv.com website.

- **Anthropologie BHLDN**

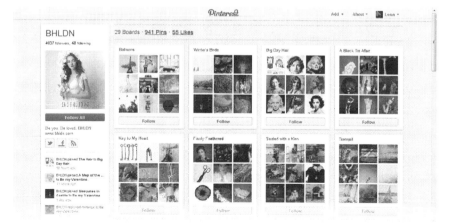

- Category: Wedding Apparel, Décor, Gifts

- Pinterest URL: pinterest.com/bhldn

- What to Note: BHLDN is a strong fit with Pinterest not only because many people use Pinterest as for wedding ideas but because BHLDN is focused on a non-traditional wedding. They sell one-of-a-kind items and items with a handmade appearance that are unique enough for Pinterest users to have a sense of discovery while browsing their boards. BHLDN also highlights the value of focus. They are only about weddings. When Pinterest users follow BHLDN, they are promised a source for wedding design inspiration. BHLDN upholds this promise by covering all aspects of a wedding regardless of whether BHLDN sells those products or services; many boards serve simply to spark ideas rather than sell products at all.

- **Michaels Stores**

o   Category: Media, Media Personality

o   Pinterest URL: pinterest.com/michaelsstores

o   What to Note: Michael's is an excellent example of landing
    page design. By clicking on an image of a craft project in
    Pinterest, the user Is taken directly to a page where they have
    not only a description of the product but step-by-step
    instructions and the ability to buy all items required for the
    craft project. They have also fully integrated the "Pin It"
    button into the Michaels.com website. Michael's has a larger
    number of boards but organizes them effectively around
    different hobbies (scrapbooking, jewelry-making, and
    needlepoint) and projects (parties, gift wrapping, organizing)
    so that hobbyists can follow only their passionate interests.

CHAPTER 3: PINTEREST MARKETING TACTICS

Getting Started

As the focus of this book is Pinterest marketing, this guide already assumes you have created an account on Pinterest and know how to do the following:

- Create an account and login

- Create a board

- Pin an item to a board

- View other pins and follow them

If you don't already know how to do these things, it will only take you about 15 minutes to learn. You can refer to the "Pinning 101" section of the Pinterest help screen to get up and running:

pinterest.com/about/help/

Currently, Pinterest is still invitation-only but invites are easy to get by signing up for the waiting list (you will get an invite in a few days), asking a friend on Pinterest, or you can email us at *invites@pinbliss.com* and we will send you one.

Marketing Tactics Overview

On a daily basis, your operational activities on Pinterest will revolve around 5 things:

- Board Organization

- Pin Content

- Pin Copy

- Link Conversion

- Getting Followers with Pinterest

- Getting Followers with Other Channels

We will go into detailed techniques and tactics for each of these tasks to optimize effectiveness for your marketing goals.

Board Organization

Board Organization is the art of organizing all your pins into groups. Good board organization makes it easier for others to find the pins that interest them and to follow only those boards that matter to them. Our board organization techniques focus on getting the right number of boards, picking good board titles, and making sure that Pinterest users who look at the boards on your profile are encouraged to follow you.

Pinterest boards for Better Homes and Gardens (pinterest.com/bhg)

- **Move your most popular boards to the top**. Occasionally rearrange your boards so that the most popular and visually appealing boards are at the top. When people click through to your profile to decide if they want to follow your boards, the first thing they will see are the boards at the top – they may not keep scrolling if they don't see something they like at first glance. To rearrange your boards, go to your own page by clicking your username from the top menu and click the "Rearrange Boards" button.

- **Name your boards so that the topic is clear**. Quirky and fun names are great for showing personality but don't do it if it's not obvious what to expect in the board. PInterest users will decide whether to follow your board based on whether it matches their interests. If they can't tell what your board contains from the name, they won't follow it.

- **Build at least 8 boards with 9 pins each**. The strategy here is simply to make sure your profile page looks full of content and actively updated. Take a look at the example Pinterest board above for Better Homes and Gardens. When someone clicks on your username to view your profile, their first impression is the top 6 or 8 boards "above the fold" (before they need to scroll down). If you have enough boards to fill the screen and each board has at least 9 visually impactful images within it, your profile will look more exciting and encourage more people to follow you.

- **Limit the number of boards by your ability to update them**. There is no hard and fast rule on the maximum number of boards. While there are successful Pinterest accounts with a very large number of boards, I would recommend limiting the number of boards based on the time and resources you have to update them. If people who follow your boards don't ever receive any new pins from you, you're not adding any value and they have no reason to follow you. If you're pinning regularly but can't add a pin to every board at least once a week, consider having fewer boards.

- **No empty boards**. Never create an empty board as a placeholder until you have the first image to put in it. Empty boards make your account look abandoned or incomplete.

- **Choose board categories that are popular**. People repin things that they think will fit in one of their own boards. This means that if it doesn't fit into one of the categories or topics they are pinning about themselves, it may end up not being repinned even if they love your pin. To get an idea of the most popular categories for pinning, start by clicking the "Everything" menu in the top toolbar and looking at the categories. You don't need to exactly mimic the "Everything" menu categories like "DIY & Crafts," "Women's Apparel," and "Travel & Places," but if your board categories don't fit into any of those categories and you aren't getting board followers, you may want to experiment with different categories.

Pinners you follow · Everything ▾ · Videos · Popular · Gifts ▾

Architecture	Kids
Art	My Life
Cars & Motorcycles	Women's Apparel
Design	Men's Apparel
DIY & Crafts	Outdoors
Education	People
Film, Music & Books	Pets
Fitness	Photography
Food & Drink	Print & Posters
Gardening	Products
Geek	Science & Nature
Hair & Beauty	Sports
History	Technology
Holidays	Travel & Places
Home Decor	Wedding & Events
Humor	Other

crust made from cauliflow
REDIBLE...best discovery e

Samye Joplin Young
Lobue onto Yum ideas

Pin Content

On Pinterest, your value to others is curation. Like a buyer for a hip department store, a fashion magazine editor, or the curator for a world-famous art museum, your job is to scour the world to bring only the very best to your customers, readers, or visitors. There are a number of strategies for making sure that you perform this curation role well to attract followers and keep your existing followers happy.

- **Pin, don't just repin.** There is a dramatic difference in the number of repins, likes, and followers you get when you pin your own content rather than just repinning something you saw on Pinterest. There are a lot of popular pins that show up again and again on Pinterest and people have already seen a lot of the repinned content already. When you pin something new that you

43

found yourself on the web or content you created, you've added real value to Pinterest and it will get noticed a lot easier.

- **Don't pin everything.** Remember that your role on Pinterest is that of a curator. People follow you because you are filtering all the content in the world to bring them the very best of some category. If you pin everything in sight, you're just contributing to the information overload and you're not adding any value. Only pin the best of the best. While "best" is subjective, if your followers consistently see low quality pins from you, they'll stop following.

- **Don't just pin your own products and services.** If you're laser-focused on marketing your own brand, products, and services, it may be tempting to only pin your own branded content. Don't do this. You want to expose your brand to people who have never seen or heard of you before. The most effective way to do this is to first attract a following of people who love the lifestyle or category you're promoting – and only then introduce them to your brand. For example, if you are Amy's Bridal Gowns, you want to first attract people who are planning weddings and not just those who are already aware of your product line. One way to do this is to pin about wedding design ideas – flowers, hair, dream locations, makeup. Then, you can also include bridal gowns and include your products. While you don't need to be so fair that you pin products from your direct competitors, you should consider pinning from sources beyond your own site so that your visitors know that you are bringing them the very best from across the web and not just your own brand. This will encourage more people to follow you and provide you an audience in the future if you want to extend your products and services into new categories.

- **Experiment with different image sizes**. Most images on the web are wider than they are long. One way to get more attention for your pins is to choose images that are longer than they are wide. This type of "skyscraper" format is advantageous because of the way Pinterest does page layout – your images will be visible longer as a user scrolls down a long list of images.

- **Do competitive research**. One quick way to find out what is popular for repinning is to look at competitors. Use the Source URL technique (explained in more detail in the "Pinterest Tools" section) to view the type and most popular content that is being repinned on a competitor's website. Consider pinning similar content as it is likely to be in categories that the Pinterest community is most interested in pinning to their own boards.

- **Choose pins that fall within popular categories**. Even if your pin is visually stunning and loved by other Pinterest users, they won't repin if most of them don't already have a board that your pin fits within. To get an idea of the most popular categories on Pinterest, start by clicking the "Everything" menu in the top toolbar and looking at the categories. Also, keep an eye on the type of pins that show up most frequently when you select "Popular" from the menu.

- **Only pin visually stunning content**. Your pin image is going to be featured on a long scrolling list alongside hundreds of other images. Pinterest users will quickly scroll through these images to find something that jumps out at them. To even have a chance of getting noticed, your image needs to visually pop. Consider composition, color, perspective, and recognizable faces as important criteria in choosing which images to pin. If your image doesn't stand out, look for a different image.

- **Add variety to your pins**. Don't pin nearly identical things all at once to the same board or your audience will be overwhelmed and stop following you. Especially for products, don't pin the green model, light green model, blue model, and 20 different variants of the same product in rapid succession. Pick your one favorite to pin.

- **Don't oversell**. Think of Pinterest as the very top of the purchase funnel... it's about discovering new things. The decision to buy comes a little bit later and can happen on your landing page once the Pinterest user decides to click through on the pin image. Focus within Pinterest on making the user curious and emotionally excited about the product or service. Don't try to turn your Pinterest image into a small ad with prominent branding, comparisons, or ad copy. The PInterest audience doesn't want their discovery process to be filled with overt advertising and it won't help you sell.

- **Pick the right products and services for Pinterest**. If you find you want to add text into your image because your product needs more education and explanation to understand, it may not be the right product for Pinterest. If no matter how you photograph the product, you can't make it visually interesting or emotionally exciting, it may be the wrong product for Pinterest. You may want to focus instead on brand values rather than promoting the products directly. Refer back to the "What Brands, Products, and Services Can You Most Effectively Promote on Pinterest?" section for selection criteria.

- **Pin what you know**. You can't fake passion. In order to be a great curator, you have to genuinely love what you're pinning and understand the category. If you don't, find someone else to contribute to the board – you can even invite someone from the Pinterest community. Your followers who really do love the category will be able to tell the difference.

Pin Copy

When you create a pin, you have the opportunity to write a description along with the image. Given the visual focus of Pinterest, you want the image to do the real work and to keep your description short. However, a few techniques can help you get noticed by more Pinterest users and search engines.

- **Use hashtags**. Just like on Twitter, you can use hashtags in your descriptions. A hashtag is nothing more than a list of keywords with a "#" character in front of each one. These hashtags make it easier for someone using the search box in Pinterest to find pins related to a specific topic. For example, if you were really interested in finding pins about necklaces, you might search for "#necklace" in the search box. You can add multiple hash tags but don't use more than 3 or it will just look like spam and make your comment hard to read. Since the purpose is search optimization, I would use only hashtags that others are likely to search on. Do a quick search in the search box for a hashtag you want to use; if it doesn't return any results you may want to choose a different hashtag.

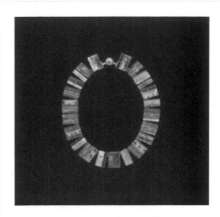

Necklace by Earl Pardon, 1989:
Cloisonne enamel on silver. #Necklace
#Jewelry #Earl_Pardon #Cloisonne

59 likes 4 comments 148 repins

- **Don't write a lot of copy**. Pinterest is visual. Most Pinterest users will rapidly scroll down a long gallery of images to find something that interests them and will not carefully read the descriptions. Don't write more than a few words in your description. If your image needs a lot of explanation to make sense, choose a different image rather than writing a long description.

- **Don't write overt sales copy**. Let the image sell itself. Don't attempt to articulate a comprehensive list of benefits, detailed comparison with competitive products, or any other copy that might be misconstrued as overt advertising. Instead, write something that peaks curiosity, and highlights the emotional appeal of the product. A simple comment about how the image makes you feel is great technique. Leave the rest of your messaging for when the user click's through to your landing page.

- **Add a price if it's a value**. The Pinterest demographic is value-conscious. If the product or service you are promoting is exceptionally priced, you can add a price in the description. In order to do this, just put a number with a $ or £ in front. Pinterest will automatically detect the price in your description and add a price banner on top of your image (see example below). This has the added benefit of adding your pin to the gifts category so that users can search for gifts by price range.

Sample pin with a $56.00 price

Link Conversion

In order for Pinterest to drive sales or traffic to your web properties, it's critical that your pins correctly link to your site or landing pages. You can also use affiliate links to get commissions on traffic that you drive to other sites. On Pinterest, the community might already be pinning about your brand, products, and services without your knowledge and not correctly linking back to you so you may also want to work to reclaim those missing or misdirected links!

- **Link pins back to your website, landing page and use affiliate links**. When you create a pin with the "+Add" button on the top menu, you will be prompted to enter an URL for your pin. You can enter links here that point to your website or landing pages. If you are an affiliate marketer, you can also use affiliate links to get commissions for sales that you helped drive.

- If you used the "Pin It" Browser button, Pinterest will create the link for you automatically. However, if you want to add an affiliate link instead or want to correct the link, you can edit your pins by hovering your mouse over your pin and clicking the "Edit" button to change the link.

Edit Pin

Description	Zip Bed by AsHome	
Link	http://www.ashome.it/Night/Letti/product.php	
Board	Home Design	
Delete	Delete Pin	

Save Pin

- **Claim pins from other Pinterest users**. You may already be on Pinterest and not know it. Other users may have already pinned images or videos from your website and other social media. In many cases, however, they may have linked to third-party blogs, press articles, or photo galleries instead of linking back to you. Unfortunately, Pinterest does not yet offer any shortcuts for reclaiming your links. The only way to do this now is to go to the Pinterest search box and find your pins by manually searching for your product names, brand names, campaign names, product keywords, and product categories and visually combing for your images and videos. If you find something that belongs to you and is not properly attributed or linked, you can message the pinner. Pinterest etiquette (pinterest.com/about/etiquette/) encourages users to credit the source so you will probably find pinners to be cooperative if you approach them in a friendly and non-threatening manner.

- **Take advantage of SEO benefits**. For those concerned with search engine optimization, Pinterest provides a do-follow link which can provide meaningful SEO benefits when linking from Pinterest to your site. Personally, I believe there is risk that Pinterest may eventually stop this practice to protect their own search ranking so there may be a limited window of opportunity here.

- **Add a link into the description**. In addition to the main link from your image, you can also add another link in the description. This second link does not need to be the same as your main image link. To do this, you just simply type a URL (with or without the http://) and Pinterest will automatically detect this and display a link.

- **Integrate with online campaigns**. If you are running online promotions, social media campaigns, or simply want to drive traffic to other social media channels, remember that you can pin images with links to Facebook pages, promotional pages with discounts, campaigns on other social networks, or other offers.

Remember, however, that other users may pin these images to their boards and you may want to plan ahead so that these links do not break after the promotion is over.

- **Align your pin and landing page**. In order to maximize conversion from Pinterest into a sale or long-term traffic to your site, you want to be sure that when a user clicks on your pin that the image in the pin and the linked page are consistent and provides the content the Pinterest user is expecting. A pin of a delicious casserole should take you to a page with the recipe and not some other type of content. You should also be sure that the linked page (the landing page) makes sense to a Pinterest user who has not visited the rest of your website. It should be a standalone page that offers opportunities for purchase, has a full description and other information needed for the user to evaluate the product for purchase. Refer to the Michaels Stores example in the "Case Studies" section for a good example.

- **Use permalinks**. Be sure you have a permanent URL for your image and landing page. If your URLs change, they won't change automatically on Pinterest. While you can edit your links to your own pins on Pinterest, you may break links that others have used to pin directly onto their own boards.

Getting Followers with Pinterest

Of course, great pins aren't very useful for marketing if nobody sees them. On Pinterest, what's important isn't just getting followers to your account (the total number of followers visible on your profile), but also followers to individual boards. Many people on Pinterest choose to follow boards rather than accounts. The techniques for getting more followers involve following others and engaging with the larger Pinterest community.

- **Follow, follow, follow**. Follow as many people as you can who have similar interests to your board content. Start by doing a search in the Pinterest search box for keywords related to your product category. For example, if you are a travel agency, search for "travel," "vacation," "hotel," "getaway", etc. The search results will return a list of Pins, Boards, and People that are relevant to your keyword (selectable from the links immediately below the search box). For pins, click on the names of the pinner underneath each pin and follow them. For boards and people, simply click the "Follow" buttons.

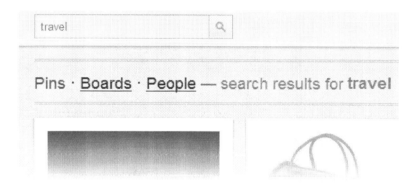

Search results show Pins, Boards, and People which you can select from the links below the search box.

Travel time

13 likes 1 comment 142 repins

Susan McElroy onto KEEP
CALM

Susan McElroy

164 followers, **190** following

Follow All

For pin search results, click on a pinner's Name and click the "Follow All" button on their profile.

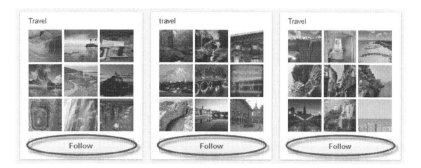

For board search results, click the "Follow" buttons.

- **Follow back people who follow you**. From your profile page, you can see the number of followers you have underneath your name. If you mouse over this number, you can click a link to see a list of who is following you. From the list of followers, you can quickly click the "Follow" buttons to follow back everyone who is following you. To take this one step further, you can also follow the followers of your followers. To do this, click the image of a person on your list of followers to go to their profile page. Then, click the number of followers under *their* name to see their followers. Pinterest does not currently recommend users to follow so you have to do this manually.

- **"Mention" other users you want to follow you**. Use "mentions" in your comments or pin descriptions to get the attention of someone you want to follow you. A "mention" works similarly to Twitter or Facebook. While writing a comment or pin description, type a "@" character while writing a description or comment and a drop-down menu will appear to allow you to select a user. You can only mention users for whom you are already following at least one board. The user mentioned will get an email notification and the mention will automatically be linked back to their profile when it appears in the pin.

photo wall

Repinned onto **DIY Crafts** from designspirationsk.com

@Caitlin Cantrell An idea for your living room

Comment

- **Repin.** Repinning is a great way to show appreciation for another user and encourage them to follow you in return. Of course, this needs to work hand-in-hand with your content strategy. You shouldn't repin just to get someone to follow you. Only repin something if it fits within your boards and meets your curation standards.

- **"Like" pins from users you want to follow you but whose pins are off-topic for your boards**. There are two ways to express appreciation for another Pinterest user's pin -- you can either repin or "like" a pin. When you either like or repin another user's pin, they will get an email notification and it will appear in their activity feed. This attention will sometimes encourage them to follow you. In general, repin if you think the pin belongs on your boards and "like" otherwise.

- **Invite others to contribute to your board**. Another way to get someone's attention is to collaborate with them. You can invite another Pinterest user to actually contribute pins to one of your boards as long as you are following at least one of their boards. You can edit your board so that "Who can pin?" is set to Me + Contributors. Since collaboration on boards is not yet that popular, this can be a clever way to break through the noise to get an influential pinner to notice you. They will get an email with your invitation but may opt out and choose not to collaborate with you.

Edit Board / Travel

Title	Travel
Description	
Who can pin?	⊙ 👤 Just Me ○ 👥 Me + Contributors
Category	Travel & Places ▼
Delete	**Delete Board**

Save Settings

Getting Followers with Other Channels

If you've already built a following on your website or other social networks, you should certainly leverage that in building a following on Pinterest. By using tools available from Pinterest, you can expose your Pinterest profile on your blog or website and provide users with an easy way to share images and videos they find on your site with Pinterest.

- **Reach out to influential Pinterest users, websites, and bloggers**. Can think of a creative way to partner with an influential blog or website for your target audience? Think of ways to cross-pin complementary products and services, share the cost and effort of a joint campaign, or cross-promote your Pinterest, social media, and web properties. Reach out to influential websites, bloggers, and Pinterest users who may be in adjacent or complementary categories to the lifestyle you are promoting on Pinterest.

- **Add a Follow button to your web pages**. On your blog or other web pages, you can put a "Follow" button that users can click to easily follow you on Pinterest. You can get more details in the "Pinterest Tools" section or at pinterest.com/about/goodies.

  FOLLOW ME ON *Pinterest*

- **Add a Pin It button next to images and videos you want shared on Pinterest**. Next to product pages or other images and video that you think will be appreciated by the Pinterest community, you can add a Pin It button to encourage users to share the image on their boards. You can get more details in the "Pinterest Tools" section or at pinterest.com/about/goodies.

  Pin it 5

- **Link your Facebook account**. If you have already built a strong following on Facebook, you can leverage this to grow your Pinterest following. In the top menu bar, you can select "Settings" in the menu labeled with your username. By clicking on the "Find Facebook Friends on Pinterest" you can invite some or all of your friends to join Pinterest. You should click the "Follow All" button to follow all existing Facebook friends that are already on Pinterest. There is also an option to "Add Pinterest to Facebook Timeline." If you slide this option to "ON," your Pinterest activity will be posted to your Facebook timeline. You should consider whether you want your pins automatically posted to Facebook carefully. Depending on the relevancy of your Pinterest pins to your entire Facebook audience and the frequency of your pins, there is a risk of oversharing that will alienate your Facebook audience. However, if you believe that a stream of visually exciting images would not overwhelm your audience and are aligned with the topics you already post on Facebook, this can be a very valuable feature.

Facebook	**ON** Link to Facebook
	ON Add Pinterest to Facebook Timeline
	Find Facebook Friends on Pinterest
Twitter	**ON** Link to Twitter

- **Make your Pinterest profile visible to search engines**. To get the broadest exposure possible, you will want to allow search engines to index your Pinterest profile so that it can be discovered in Google search and other search services. To do, this set the Visibility slider to "ON" under the Settings menu option.

Visibility **ON** Hide your Pinterest profile from search engines

Pinterest Tools

If you are a Community Manager, Marketing Manager, or other Social Media expert, there are a few tools that are essential to managing your boards and community on Pinterest. These tools will make it easier for you to pin and repin as well as making it easier for others to pin content on your website and blogs.

- **Source URL**. One of the most useful competitive research tools is a URL rather than something you need to download. You can go to the URL pinterest.com/source/*domain* to get a visual list of all the pins that originated from the specified *domain* name. So, if you want to see what people pinned from etsy.com, you enter the URL pinterest.com/source/etsy.com in your browser. For each piece of content, you will also be able to gauge popularity from how many repins it got.

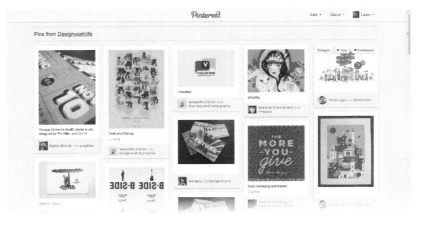

Search result from *pinterest.com/source/designworklife.com*

- **"Pin It" Browser Button**. To make it easier to pin images you find on the web, you can add a "Pin It" button to your browser's

Bookmarks Toolbar. Once installed, you can just press the "Pin It" button whenever you see something on a web page that you want to pin. You will be able to select the image you want on the page and it will automatically provide the appropriate link back to the source page.

Installation is an easy drag-and-drop process. Just go to pinterest.com/about/goodies in your preferred browser for instructions.

- **"Pin It" button**. If you want to encourage more visitors to your blog or website to pin content to Pinterest, you can easily add a "Pin It" button to your web pages. To do this, you will need to grab a snippet of HTML code from Pinterest at pinterest.com/about/goodies.

- **Follow button**. If you want to get more followers, you can add a Follow button on your website or blogs so that you can follow you with just a click. You can get the HTML code for this button from Pinterest at pinterest.com/about/goodies.

FOLLOW ME ON *Pinterest*

- **Pinterest Mobile App**. The Pinterest iPhone app allows you to browse, pin, repin, and take photos for pins on the go. You

can install it from the iTunes Store by searching for
"pinterest."

- **RSS Feed**. Each Pinterest account also has a RSS feed
  associated with it at the URL
  pinterest.com/*username*/feed.rss. For example, if your
  username is "leoncho", your feed URL is
  pinterest.com/leoncho/feed.rss. Other people can use
  existing RSS readers (iGoogle, Google Reader, My Yahoo!,
  Netvibes, Pageflakes, etc.) to get a live feed of your pins. If
  you'd like to share your Pinterest feed with other users on
  your blog or website, you can go to feedburner.google.com
  and "burn" your Pinterest feed URL. The Feedburner site will
  provide you with the additional tools you need.

Leon Cho

Clear Canoe
Tuesday, January 24, 2012 12:33 AM

Clear Canoe

Backyard Scrabble
Friday, January 20, 2012 9:41 PM

Backyard Scrabble

photo wall
Friday, January 20, 2012 9:37 PM

Conclusion

You recognized the potential of Pinterest early. As Pinterest rocketed onto the list of most visited social networks, you recognized that something was different about Pinterest. It wasn't like the other social networks. The appeal to women and their families, the explosion of visual images instead of blocks of text, the showcase of aspirational lifestyles... this was no Facebook or Twitter.

Now you understand why Pinterest is so transformative. Not only is it a different model for the users, it's also a different model for marketers. Even though there is no overt advertising on the surface, the marketers with the insight into this new model are finding that it can be an even better way to build brands, communicate with affinity groups, and drive sales and traffic. They're doing it – and now so can you.

But in order to make Pinterest work effectively, you have to know what brands, products, and services fit with the Pinterest demographic and marketing strategies. You've learned how to build a strategic brief that's appropriate for an environment that rewards rapid change and flexibility. You've also learned specific Pinterest marketing tactics for board organization, pin selection and copy, getting followers, cross-promoting Pinterest with your other web properties, and the tools you need to manage Pinterest on a daily basis.

You're ready. You have a head start on making the most of Pinterest . Pinterest is growing by leaps and bounds and this will be an exciting journey. Please join our community of Pinterest marketers on www.pinbliss.com as we all continue to learn and grow together. Happy pinning!

About The Author

Leon Cho is a technology executive who has worked at the intersection of online marketing and product management for over 15 years. He is a former VP/GM at Match.com (Chemistry.com division), General Manager at Real Networks, and has held senior roles at AOL and Netscape. He has an MBA from the University of Chicago in Marketing and Finance where he received the university's Marketing Concentration scholarship. He has dual degrees from the University of California at Berkeley in Computer Science and Applied Mathematics.

I would love to hear from you if you have any questions, feedback, or suggestions on this book. Please also join me on PinBliss.com for updates from the rapidly growing Pinterest Marketing community!

Web: www.PinBliss.com
Pinterest: pinterest.com/leoncho
Web: about.me/leoncho
Twitter: @leoncho
Email: leon@pinbliss.com

Made in the USA
Lexington, KY
06 November 2012